Simon Bent
ACCOMPLICES

OBERON BOOKS
LONDON

First published in 2000 by Oberon Books Ltd.
(incorporating Absolute Classics)
521 Caledonian Road, London N7 9RH
Tel: 020 7607 3637 / Fax: 020 7607 3629

e-mail: oberon.books@btinternet.com

A catalogue record for this book is available from the British Library.

ISBN: 1 84002 171 3

Cover design: Andrzej Klimowski

Typography: Richard Doust

Printed in Great Britain by Antony Rowe Ltd, Reading.

For Billie

Characters

NICKY

STUART

GARY

JOHN

PAUL

EDDIE

DOREEN

HORSLEY

Accomplices was first performed at the Crucible Theatre, Sheffield on 25th October 2000. A Crucible Theatre and Royal National Theatre Studio co-production, it had the following cast:

NICKY, James Weaver

STUART, Dave Hawkins

GARY, Laurence Mitchell

JOHN, Neil Grainger

PAUL, Kenny Doughty

EDDIE, Tom Marshall

DOREEN, Anna Keaveny

HORSLEY, Neil McCaul

Director, Paul Miller
Designer, Jackie Brooks
Lighting designer, Andy Phillips
Fight director, Terry King
Sound designer, Huw Williams

Stage manager, Stephanie Dailey
Deputy stage manager, Chris Knibbs
Assistant stage manager, Corrie Cooper
Assistant director, Arlette Kim George

(With thanks to Michael Grandage, Graham Morris, Sue Higginson, Jack Bradley, Matt Strevens, Eddie Keogh and the staff of the Crucible)

Set in the present. On and around a housing estate in the North of England.

ACT ONE

Scene 1

NICKY and STUART. NICKY is smoking.

NICKY: Tell me her name. Go on. What's she called?

STUART: I need a bag of chips.

NICKY: Can I stop at yours tonight?

STUART: What for?

NICKY: Oh, forget it.

STUART: I need a bag of chips. What's wrong with your house?

NICKY: Nothing.

STUART: So why do you want to come and stop at mine?

NICKY: I don't, alright.

STUART: Alright. It's not coming.

NICKY: It's coming.

STUART: I need a bag of chips.

NICKY stubs out his cigarette.

NICKY: Give us a fag.

STUART: You've got your own.

NICKY: I want one of yours.

STUART: Smoke your own.

NICKY: Why won't you tell me her name?

STUART: You don't know her.

NICKY: What's her name? Tell me her name.

STUART: You don't know her.

NICKY: Come on, I'd tell you.

STUART: No you bloody wouldn't.

NICKY: I would.

STUART: I'm not telling you. You'll take the piss.

NICKY: No I won't, honest I won't.

STUART: She works in that boutique on the High Street.

NICKY: A boutique.

STUART: A boutique.

NICKY: She sells clothes.

STUART: She's in the fashion business.

NICKY: She's a shop assistant.

STUART: I told you you'd take the piss.

NICKY: I'm not.

STUART: I like her, I like her a lot, she's really – really really calm.

NICKY: So you've got a lot in common.

STUART: Her names's Natalie.

NICKY: Natalie.

STUART: Yeah.

NICKY: No, I don't know her.

STUART: She comes in the pub a lot, dark hair and a roundish face.

NICKY: Oh, dark hair and a roundish face.

STUART: Yeah.

NICKY: Yeah.

STUART: Fuck off.

They both laugh.

She's really really pretty – but I don't know, I just don't know.

NICKY: Why, what's wrong with her?

STUART: I'm not sure about her teeth.

Enter GARY with a bag of shopping.

NICKY: Oh, hello Gary.

GARY: Nicky. Stuart.

NICKY: How are you?

GARY: Alright. You?

NICKY: Not so bad. You've been shopping.

GARY: Yeah. It's me mam, her legs are bad again.

STUART: We're waiting for a bus.

NICKY: (*To STUART.*) It's coming. He thinks the bus isn't coming. Stay and wait with us if you like.

GARY: No, I can't. It's me mam.

NICKY: Got any fags?

GARY: No.

NICKY: Have a fag.

NICKY gives GARY a cigarette.

Stay and have a fag with us while our bus comes.

NICKY gives GARY a light.

GARY: Ta.

STUART: (*To GARY.*) Why didn't the turkey cross the road?

GARY: Dunno.

STUART: Because it wasn't a chicken.

NICKY: Thinks he's a comedian.

STUART: How do you spell Nicky?

GARY: N – I – C – K – Y.

STUART: C – U – N – T, cunt.

NICKY: We're going into town.

STUART: I'm hungry.

NICKY: He's got worms. (*To GARY.*) Lend us a fiver.

GARY: I haven't got any money, honest.

STUART: It's not bloody coming.

NICKY: If it doesn't come within the next five minutes we'll go and throw some bricks at the Jackson's house, alright?

STUART: Yeah, alright.

NICKY: Here, you could come with us.

GARY: No, I can't.

NICKY: Oh yeah, pal of yours.

GARY: We were at school together.

NICKY: Paul Jackson. I don't like him, I don't like his family , they get right up my nose. Come and throw some bricks at his house with us.

GARY: No, I can't.

NICKY: Yeah, been shopping.

GARY: It's me mam's legs.

NICKY: What did you get?

GARY: Bread, milk, beans, cornflakes –

NICKY: Cornflakes.

STUART: Cornflakes.

GARY: Cornflakes.

STUART: We don't like cornflakes.

NICKY: He's hungry. He's always hungry. Anything else?

GARY: And half a dozen eggs.

NICKY: Right.

GARY: Right.

GARY stubs out his cigarette.

I have to go.

NICKY: You should come out with us for a drink sometime.

GARY: Yeah, alright.

NICKY: You'd like that?

GARY: Yeah, I would.

NICKY: You're not just saying it?

GARY: No, no, no – I'd really like to.

NICKY: Right, tonight, The Bell, eight thirty.

STUART: Mine's a pint of bitter and a packet of crisps.

GARY goes to exit.

NICKY: Hang about, show us your eggs.

GARY: You what?

NICKY: I said show us your eggs.

GARY: What for?

STUART: He wants to look at your eggs.

NICKY: Yeah.

GARY gives the box of eggs to NICKY.

NICKY opens the box and holds up an egg.

Big, aren't they. How much did they cost?

GARY: I don't know.

NICKY: Twenty-five pence.

GARY: Ninety.

NICKY: (*To STUART.*) Give him a quid.

STUART: What for.

NICKY: For the eggs.

STUART: I'm not giving him a quid.

NICKY: Give him a pound.

STUART gives GARY a pound.

GARY: (*To NICKY.*) Thanks.

NICKY: That's alright. Tell your mam, I hope her legs get better soon.

GARY: Yeah, I will.

NICKY: And don't forget tonight, the Bell.

GARY: No, I won't.

Exit GARY.

STUART: He won't come.

NICKY: He'll come. I'm stopping at your's tonight then.

STUART: Yeah, alright – but we're not sharing a bed.

NICKY: No, you can have the floor.

NICKY goes to exit.

STUART: Where are you going?

NICKY: To get a bag of chips.

Scene 2

JOHN and PAUL.

JOHN is asleep on the floor, a sidelamp by his side and a book.

PAUL is sitting on a chair smoking a cigarette and watching JOHN.

PAUL: John. John. Wake up Johnny, it's me Johnny. I'm back, I'm home. John.

He kicks JOHN gently. JOHN wakes.

JOHN: Paul.

PAUL: Quiet, it's late.

JOHN: You're back.

PAUL: I don't want to wake them.

JOHN: When did you get back?

PAUL: Just now.

JOHN: How long have you been back?

PAUL: Just now.

JOHN: You're late.

PAUL: My train broke down and I had to walk from the station.

JOHN: We weren't expecting you.

PAUL: You were waiting up.

JOHN: I was reading and I fell asleep.

PAUL: I said I was coming.

JOHN: You didn't ring.

PAUL: I couldn't.

JOHN: You should've rang.

PAUL: You were waiting.

JOHN: Give us a ciggy.

PAUL: You don't smoke.

JOHN: I started.

PAUL throws a packet of ten cigarettes to JOHN.

How did you get in?

PAUL: The back door.

JOHN: It wasn't bolted.

PAUL: It wasn't bolted.

JOHN: Jesus, I was meant to bolt it.

JOHN holds up the cigarettes.

They're all wet.

PAUL: It's raining. I got chased coming home.

JOHN: Are you alright?

PAUL: Yeah. They got my bag.

JOHN: But you're alright.

PAUL: I lost my bag. I took a short cut across the playing fields and down past the Bell – and they were all coming out – Nicky Tanner, Stuart Earnshaw and Gary Clifton.

JOHN: Gary Clifton.

PAUL: Yeah.

JOHN: I thought he was a mate.

PAUL: Don't tell mam.

JOHN: No, I won't.

PAUL: Don't tell her Johnny.

JOHN: I won't.

PAUL ruffles JOHN's hair.

PAUL: Good lad.

JOHN: Get off. Go on, give us a drag.

PAUL gives a cigarette to JOHN.

Cheers.

PAUL: I lost my bag.

JOHN: There's nothing left. How's college?

PAUL: I fell down a hole.

JOHN: You what.

PAUL: You were waiting up.

JOHN: No I wasn't. How's college?

PAUL: Alright.

JOHN: Got a girlfriend?

PAUL: Johnny.

JOHN: I'm only asking. Well have you?

PAUL: You know. You?

JOHN: You must be joking.

They both laugh.

PAUL: How is she?

JOHN: Alright. Dad's on some new tablets for his heart.

PAUL: So, you're sleeping down here now are you, on the floor?

JOHN: I was reading.

PAUL: What are you reading?

JOHN: Before the Beginning. It's about the Universe.

PAUL: You were waiting.

JOHN: I was reading.

PAUL: You were waiting.

PAUL tickles JOHN and they roll about the floor.

JOHN: Get off – stop it – stop it will you, get off.

PAUL: Sssh. You'll wake them.

JOHN: You fell down a hole.

PAUL: Yeah.

They laugh.

JOHN puts on a Kangol hat, as worn by Oasis.

JOHN: I knew you'd be back tonight – Dad said you'd be back tomorrow, but I knew.

PAUL: What are you wearing that for?

JOHN: I like it.

PAUL: Take it off.

JOHN: It's cool.

PAUL: Johnny.

JOHN: Alright.

JOHN takes off his hat.

PAUL: You need a haircut.

JOHN: I'm not having it shaved again.

PAUL: I like it shaved.

JOHN: Well I don't and it's my head right. Get your own head shaved this time.

PAUL: I like rubbing my hand up and down the back of your head.

JOHN: Rub your own head.

Three short sharp bursts of a doorbell.

Silence.

A long insistent ringing of the doorbell.

Silence.

They've gone.

A rapid quick-fire volley of dull thuds at the front door.

Pause.

A further rapid volley of dull thuds at the front door.

Silence.

Enter EDDIE violently brandishing a poker. He switches on the big light.

EDDIE: Yaargh!

PAUL: Arrgh!

JOHN: Arrgh!

EDDIE: Bloody hell.

PAUL: Hello, Dad.

EDDIE: What are you doing here?

PAUL: I've come home.

EDDIE: (*Shouting off.*) Doreen – it's John and Paul. (*To boys.*) We thought you were burglars.

Enter DOREEN.

PAUL: Mam.

DOREEN: Paul.

EDDIE: I'll look out front.

Exit EDDIE.

DOREEN: What are you doing home?

PAUL: I live here.

DOREEN: Where have you been?

JOHN: His train broke down.

DOREEN: You should've rang.

PAUL: I couldn't.

DOREEN: You should've rang, we weren't expecting you.

PAUL kisses her on cheek.

There's nothing hot, I've got nothing hot –

PAUL: It's alright, I'm not hungry.

DOREEN: You're covered in mud.

PAUL: I'm alright.

DOREEN: I'll open a tin of soup.

PAUL: It's alright.

DOREEN: Have something cold.

PAUL: Mam, I don't want anything.

DOREEN: Where's your bag?

PAUL: What bag? Oh yeah, I left it on the train.

DOREEN: You'd lose your head if it wasn't attached to your shoulders.

JOHN: Yeah, he hasn't got a brain.

DOREEN: You've been smoking.

JOHN: No I haven't.

DOREEN: (*To PAUL.*) You've been giving your brother cigarettes.

JOHN: Mam.

DOREEN: It's bad enough you killing yourself –

PAUL: I'm not killing myself.

DOREEN: Without trying to kill your brother as well. I'll get you some soup. We didn't think you were coming, when you never rang, you should have rang – I didn't know what had happened, anything could have happened –

PAUL: I'm alright.

DOREEN: You're soaked to the bone and you've started your brother smoking again.

JOHN: Mam.

DOREEN: Get your brother a towel.

Enter EDDIE.

EDDIE: Eggs.

DOREEN: Now Johnny.

JOHN: Do I have to?

DOREEN: Yes.

EDDIE: The front door's covered in eggs.

DOREEN: (*To JOHN.*) Now.

JOHN: Why's it always me?

Exit JOHN.

EDDIE: Broken eggs, all over the front door. That's the third time this month.

DOREEN: You go back to bed and I'll clean it up. (*Shouting off.*) Top drawer, one of the big ones. (*To EDDIE.*) He's soaked. Well don't just stand there, get your clothes off.

EDDIE: I'll get the hose on it tomorrow.

DOREEN: I've said I'll do it.

EDDIE: Tomorrow.

DOREEN: Tonight. Take your clothes off.

EDDIE: Leave it till tomorrow.

DOREEN: I'll do it now. Get those wet things off or you'll catch your death.

PAUL takes off his jacket.

(*Shouting off.*) John.

EDDIE: I'll bolt the kitchen.

Exit EDDIE.

DOREEN: How did you get mud on your jacket?

PAUL: It's nothing.

DOREEN: And your shirt?

PAUL: It's nothing.

DOREEN: Everything off.

PAUL undresses down to his socks and loud boxer shorts. DOREEN watches.

Look at you.

PAUL: I slipped.

DOREEN: How did you get covered in mud?

PAUL: I fell down a hole.

DOREEN: No you didn't.

PAUL: I did.

DOREEN: You didn't.

PAUL: I did, I fell down a hole, it was dark I wasn't looking where I was going and I fell down a hole.

DOREEN: What did you do that for?

PAUL: I don't know, I didn't do it on purpose it just happened.

Enter JOHN with a towel. He sees PAUL in his boxers.

JOHN: Rock on, Tommy.

JOHN throws the towel to DOREEN.

DOREEN: I said a big one.

JOHN: That's big enough for him.

DOREEN: And take that hat off.

JOHN: I like wearing it.

DOREEN: Not in the house. You don't see your father wearing his hat round the house do you?

JOHN: I wouldn't be seen dead in a hat like his.

He looks at PAUL in his boxer shorts.

Where d'you get those from?

DOREEN: We don't want to know. And your socks.

PAUL takes off his socks.

JOHN: I bet they get all the girls going.

DOREEN throws the towel to PAUL.

DOREEN: Go and get your brother a dressing gown.

JOHN: What for?

DOREEN: Because I say.

PAUL: Because you've got all your clothes on.

JOHN: Why me, why's it always me?

DOREEN: And take that hat off.

Exit JOHN.

And the shorts.

PAUL: Mam.

DOREEN: Don't be silly.

PAUL wraps the towel round his waist. DOREEN gathers up his clothes.

What happened, something happened?

PAUL: Nothing happened.

DOREEN: The shorts.

PAUL pulls down his boxers from under the towel and kicks them off.

DOREEN picks them up.

Enter EDDIE.

EDDIE: I've locked up in the kitchen.

DOREEN: Something's happened and he's not telling us.

PAUL: Nothing's happened.

EDDIE: Leave the boy alone.

DOREEN: Something's happened.

EDDIE: Doreen.

DOREEN: He's got mud on his clothes and he's left his bag on the train.

EDDIE: Just leave him alone. It's a waste of good eggs.

Silence.

Night then.

PAUL: Night, Dad.

EDDIE: Oh, don't let the tap run in the sink – the pipe's broke and I've had to improvise until I can get to a shop.

PAUL: Right, Dad.

EDDIE: Right. Night.

DOREEN: I'll be up in a minute.

Exit EDDIE.

I'll put these in the wash. I've got some ham, I'll make you a ham sandwich. Do you want mustard?

PAUL: No.

DOREEN: (*Shouting off.*) Johnny! You'll catch your death. How about some tomato?

PAUL: Just mustard.

Exit DOREEN.

Scene 3

NICKY, GARY and STUART downstage right. NICKY eating a bag of chips. JOHN upstage right reading.

JOHN: (*As if talking to someone just offstage.*) What we call the Universe, right.

STUART: You still want her?

NICKY: No I don't.

JOHN: Well it might not be the Universe.

STUART: Did she ever make you beg for it?

NICKY: What? No.

STUART: Liar. You begged.

NICKY: No I never.

GARY: It's going to rain.

STUART: I don't mean you used the word – I mean you begged for it, she had you begging for it.

NICKY: Shut it right.

STUART: Alright.

GARY: It is, it's going to rain.

JOHN: The Universe, our Universe right, well it might be just one of millions upon millions of countless others – all contained within one big giant Universe.

Enter PAUL with a postcard upstage right.

Other Universes in which the laws are different, all collapsing towards the Big Crunch.

PAUL: Yeah.

JOHN: Who's your postcard from?

PAUL: No one.

PAUL lies on the floor and reads the card upstage left.

NICKY: In America, when a Hell's Angel finishes with a woman they gut them and then feed them to the crocodiles. And the women, they become their possessions, to do with as they want.

STUART: That must be nice for the women.

NICKY: Yeah. To sell, to love and to kill.

STUART: It means they don't have to think.

GARY: Who don't have to think?

STUART: The women, there's no need for them to think.

NICKY: Yeah.

STUART: I've never been dumped.

NICKY: I wasn't dumped. It was me that dumped her, right?

STUART: Right.

NICKY: She had a perm and it put me right off.

JOHN: Show us your card.

PAUL: No.

JOHN: What's she called?

PAUL: I'll hit you if you don't stop it.

GARY: What was it like? What was prison like?

STUART: It wasn't prison.

NICKY: It's nearer than you've ever got.

STUART: I came to visit.

GARY: What was it like?

NICKY: Alright.

GARY: What was the food like?

NICKY: Alright.

STUART: Better than his mam's. Give us a chip.

NICKY: Have a chip, Gary.

GARY: Thanks.

GARY takes a chip.

STUART: (*To GARY.*) How old are you?

GARY: Nineteen.

STUART: Early nineteen or late nineteen?

GARY: Nineteen and a half. How old are you?

STUART: I don't think age matters anyhow. It's not how old you are that counts.

NICKY: Here, how about this one, 'Dad dies in kinky sex experiment.'

STUART: Yeah, go on.

NICKY: Middle-aged dad dies –

STUART: Yeah.

NICKY: Dies of huge electric shock.

STUART: Right.

NICKY: When he wires his nipples and manhood to the mains, through the standard lamp in the corner of his front room and then turns himself on.

STUART: What does he do that for?

NICKY: To get an electric shock.

STUART: What for?

NICKY: It's electricity, right.

STUART: Right.

NICKY: It turns you on… D'you get it, electricity, it turns you on.

STUART: Yeah.

NICKY: Oh, forget it.

STUART: Yeah, yeah, I get it, electricity, funny.

GARY: (*To NICKY.*) But what was it like?

STUART: There's some people I'd like to electrocute.

GARY: What was it like inside?

NICKY: It's not like what you think. I'm glad I've done it but I'm not going back.

STUART: See them fry.

GARY: I'm going for a slash.

Exit GARY.

STUART: I don't like him.

NICKY: What's wrong with him?

STUART: I don't know.

NICKY: Well I like him, alright.

STUART: He laughs at your jokes.

NICKY: They're funny.

JOHN: It must be nice to get a postcard.

PAUL: Yes, it is.

STUART: Do you get paid if your dad dies, d'you get compassionate leave or something?

NICKY: From what?

STUART: From work.

NICKY: You don't work.

STUART: I work, I've worked..

NICKY: Easy boy, easy. Give us a kiss.

Enter GARY. NICKY throws a chip at STUART.

Have a chip.

JOHN: A man in Leicester says it's the end of the world next Tuesday.

PAUL: Oh yeah.

JOHN: Yeah. Show me your card.

STUART: But do you think that you do get compensation if your dad dies? It's a bit bloody hard if you don't.

JOHN: This is his second go at it. He said it was going to happen last year, and when it didn't he realised that he'd got his figures wrong. He's issued an apology with this year's prediction.

PAUL: Johnny.

JOHN: Show us your card.

PAUL: No.

JOHN: Oh go on.

PAUL: Stop it will you.

JOHN: Who's it from?

PAUL: I'll hit you.

JOHN: Show me your card.

PAUL: Just grow up.

JOHN: I will, after you've shown me your card.

PAUL goes to give JOHN the card but suddenly withholds it.

PAUL: And no reading it.

PAUL gives the card to JOHN. JOHN looks at the picture.

JOHN: (*Reading the front of card.*) Bridget Bardot.

PAUL: A French film actress.

JOHN: She's got an incredible body.

PAUL: Yeah.

JOHN: Yeah.

PAUL: Yeah.

JOHN: Astounding.

JOHN turns the card over and reads.

Julie.

PAUL: I said no reading.

JOHN: Is that her name?

PAUL: Give it back.

JOHN: Julie.

PAUL: Johnny.

JOHN: Julie.

PAUL chases JOHN for the card.

PAUL: Give it back, give it back!

PAUL gets JOHN in an armlock.

Give me my card.

JOHN: You're breaking my arm.

PAUL: Give me the card.

Enter DOREEN.

DOREEN: John –

PAUL lets go of JOHN.

Get me a bag of potatoes from the shop when you've finished, will you?

PAUL: He wouldn't give me my card.

DOREEN: I thought you were looking for a holiday job.

PAUL: I am.

DOREEN: There's a five pound note on the kitchen table.

Exit DOREEN.

JOHN offers the postcard to PAUL. Just as PAUL goes to take the card JOHN snatches it away and runs off.

PAUL: Johnny.

Exit PAUL after JOHN.

NICKY: You've got a sister.

GARY: Yeah.

NICKY: How old is she?

GARY: Sixteen.

STUART: Does she go?

NICKY: He's an animal. What's she like?

GARY: I dunno.

NICKY: Well, do you fancy her?

GARY: She's my sister.

STUART: So, what's that got to do with anything?

NICKY: Just shut it, will you! Would I like her?

GARY: I don't know.

NICKY: Would she like me?

GARY: Yeah, yeah she would.

NICKY: She sounds alright does your sister.

STUART: Yeah.

NICKY: You keep your hands off her. (*To GARY.*) He fancies his mam.

STUART: Sexy legs.

GARY: Cool jacket.

NICKY: It's my dad's. Seventies.

GARY: Smart.

NICKY: When I was a kid I was always trying on my dad's clothes – jackets, shirts, trousers, shoes – I couldn't wait till I was big enough to wear them. And now I'm bigger than him, this only just fits – bigger hands, bigger feet –

STUART: Bigger head.

NICKY: Watch it, you!

STUART: I never said anything.

NICKY: I'll have you, I will, I'm warning you.

NICKY kicks at STUART.

STUART: Come on. Go on then. I dare you.

STUART and NICKY fight.

Enter JOHN and PAUL, JOHN with a bag of potatoes.

STUART and NICKY stop fighting.

Silence.

PAUL: Gary.

GARY: Paul. John.

NICKY: Mates of yours.

GARY: We were at school together.

STUART: (*To JOHN.*) What's that?

JOHN: A bag of potatoes.

NICKY: Are you having chips? We've had chips. Do you
have chips at university?

PAUL: Come on, John.

PAUL makes to go. NICKY blocks his way.

NICKY: We were just having a friendly scrap. Do you fight?

PAUL: No.

STUART: He doesn't fight.

NICKY: Shut it. He's got no manners, eats like a pig.
We fight – it's only a game like, we're mates.

STUART: Yeah, I let him win.

NICKY: (*To JOHN.*) Thump me.

STUART: Yeah, go on thump him.

NICKY: I won't hit back, honest – I promise.

STUART: Thump him.

NICKY: On the Bible.

JOHN: You don't believe in God.

NICKY: Who says.

STUART: And even if he didn't, that doesn't mean to say
that there isn't a God, that God doesn't exist.

NICKY: Hit me.

JOHN: No.

NICKY: So you're back, back from university.

PAUL: Yeah.

NICKY: University.

STUART: University.

NICKY: What's it like?

PAUL: Alright.

NICKY: What's the food like?

PAUL: Alright.

STUART: I don't like students.

PAUL: Come on, John.

NICKY: No don't go. Here, listen to this, you'll like this. I was in the Greyhound the other night, last orders, and this bird – well she wasn't a bird she was a middle-aged woman – she comes over, puts her arm round me and says, 'How big is it then, son?' – can you believe that, she told me she was a sex and love addict, SLA – you go to university, what do you get if you put a G on the end of that?

PAUL: Slag.

NICKY: You what?

PAUL: Slag.

NICKY: That's right, it was me mam.

STUART: Are you calling his mam a slag?

PAUL: No.

JOHN: Leave him alone.

NICKY: Oh, yeah?

JOHN: Yeah.

NICKY: Your brother called my mam a slag, do you think my mam is a slag?

JOHN: No.

NICKY: Well, she is.

STUART: Yeah, his mam is a slag.

NICKY: Shut it. She's a dog, she'll shag anything that buys her a pint of cider and a packet of nuts, she's queen of the psycho's my mam.

NICKY pulls out a knife.

STUART pushes PAUL to the ground and pins him to the ground, sitting astride his back.

(*To GARY.*) Watch the end of the road. Do it, now.

Exit GARY.

(*To JOHN.*) It's a Bowie knife. Pull out your shirt.

JOHN remains still.

Pull out your shirt.

PAUL: Do as he says, John.

NICKY: He's clever.

PAUL: Just do it, Johnny.

JOHN pulls out his shirt.

NICKY: Johnny. I don't like buttons.

NICKY pulls the front of JOHN's shirt tight and cuts off the buttons.

STUART: Yeah.

Enter GARY.

34

GARY: There's a copper at the bottom of the road.

NICKY: What's he doing?

GARY: Drinking a can of coke.

He looks at PAUL and JOHN.

He's coming up the road, he's coming this way.

NICKY: (*To JOHN.*) He'll be a friend of the family. One day I'm going to stick this in your belly and rip out your guts with my teeth.

Exit NICKY and STUART. GARY follows them.

Scene 4

EDDIE with a wooden kitchen chair on its side. He is glueing the joints of the chair with wood glue.

Enter DOREEN.

DOREEN: That was your Auntie June on the phone. She's got worse and doesn't expect to make it to July.

EDDIE: What did you say?

DOREEN: I said, if she could hang on till August we might get over to see her.

EDDIE: Get me a damp cloth, will you?

DOREEN: How long does it take to buy a bag of potatoes?

EDDIE: I don't know.

DOREEN: Something's happened.

EDDIE: Nothing's happened.

DOREEN: I can feel it.

EDDIE holds tight a leg of the chair at one of its joints, squeezing it together.

EDDIE: Get me a cloth, will you?

DOREEN: I could have married the Minister of Transport.

EDDIE: It was his brother that liked you.

DOREEN: I could have married the Minister of Transport's brother.

EDDIE: That's right.

DOREEN: You should have done that in the kitchen.

Exit DOREEN.

EDDIE remains holding the chair.

Enter PAUL with a bag of potatoes.

EDDIE: Where have you been?

PAUL: To the shop.

EDDIE: Your mother's worried.

PAUL: She's always worried. What are you doing?

EDDIE: Fixing the chair.

Enter DOREEN with a cloth.

DOREEN: You took your time, what took you so long?

PAUL: Nothing.

DOREEN: Where's John?

PAUL: Upstairs.

DOREEN: You'll be late for your own funeral you will.

*DOREEN throws the cloth to EDDIE. He makes no attempt
to catch it and remains holding the chair in place. The cloth
lands at his side.*

EDDIE: Thank you.

PAUL: Here's your potatoes.

He gives DOREEN the bag of potatoes.

DOREEN: What about the change, don't I get any change?

PAUL: Oh yeah, I forgot.

EDDIE wipes the joints of the chair with the damp cloth.

PAUL gives DOREEN the change.

DOREEN: Your hands are filthy.

PAUL: Three pound seventy.

DOREEN: I'm not having you spend it on cigarettes and killing yourself.

Enter JOHN.

You've changed your shirt. What have you changed your shirt for?

JOHN: I felt like it.

EDDIE stands admiring the chair.

EDDIE: And nobody sit on that chair for at least twenty four hours.

DOREEN: What have you changed your shirt for?

JOHN: I was hot, it was hot – I was too hot.

DOREEN: You only put it on this morning.

PAUL: I like your trainers, Dad.

JOHN: Yeah, they're cool.

EDDIE: I like them as well, but your mother keeps telling me they don't fit.

DOREEN: They're too tight.

EDDIE: How do you know, you're not wearing them, are you?

DOREEN: You always have trouble with your feet.

EDDIE: There's nothing wrong with my feet.

DOREEN: Go and get your shirt and I'll put it in the wash.

JOHN: Paul got a postcard this morning.

DOREEN: I know.

JOHN: Show them your postcard, Paul.

PAUL doesn't.

Come on. What's wrong with it?

PAUL: Nothing.

PAUL holds up the card.

JOHN: Bridget Bardot. A French film actress.

DOREEN: That's nice. She hasn't got much on.

EDDIE: I'll put this chair in the kitchen.

Exit EDDIE with the chair.

DOREEN: So, who's it from then?

PAUL: A friend.

DOREEN: Oh, a friend.

JOHN: Julie.

PAUL: She's just a friend that's all.

DOREEN: Young girls now, they've got nothing in their heads, sawdust for brains, they just jump up and down and wave their fists in the air all the time and expect the world, I see them on the telly, there's nothing to them.

A young girl in Caroline Street put her baby on top of her cooker to watch the extractor fan thing go round and round, it kept it amused, and the cooker was still on and the baby died.

PAUL: Was it gas or electric?

DOREEN: Electric.

PAUL: I've never liked electricity.

DOREEN: Is that what they teach you at university?

PAUL: What?

JOHN: I like the name Julie.

DOREEN: You, go and get your shirt.

JOHN: Why, what have I done?

DOREEN: Shirt, now.

Exit JOHN.

And when was the last time you had a bath?

PAUL: I don't know. I'm not dirty.

DOREEN: Your hands are filthy.

PAUL: I fell over.

DOREEN: What did you fall over for?

PAUL: I don't know. I tripped.

DOREEN: Look at you. What kind of a girl goes out with a boy that doesn't wash?

PAUL: Mam, she's just a friend.

DOREEN: Look at you.

PAUL: I fell over. Honest.

DOREEN: I worry.

PAUL: There's no need.

Enter JOHN.

DOREEN: Where's your shirt?

JOHN: Can't find it.

Enter EDDIE wiping his hands with a hand towel.

EDDIE: Can we have custard for tea?

JOHN: I want a Chinese.

DOREEN: You'll get what you're given. (*To PAUL.*) We'll go into town tomorrow and get you some clothes to smarten you up.

EDDIE: We're not going shopping tomorrow.

DOREEN: Why not?

EDDIE: All the shops are shut, it's Sunday.

JOHN: Not in London they're not.

EDDIE: They don't believe in God in London.

DOREEN: They don't believe in God anywhere.

EDDIE: What do you want to go shopping for anyway, you went to a shop yesterday.

DOREEN: The Co-op.

EDDIE: It's a shop.

DOREEN: He needs some clothes.

JOHN: And me.

DOREEN: Where's your shirt?

JOHN: I can't find it.

DOREEN: You're hiding something. He's hiding something.

JOHN: No I'm not.

PAUL: He's not.

DOREEN: What are you hiding?

JOHN: Nothing.

DOREEN: So what took you so long at the shops?

PAUL: Nothing, we were just slow that's all. I stopped for a fag, alright.

DOREEN: Go and wash your hands.

PAUL: Oh, Mam.

DOREEN: You've been out and you fell over, a grown man.

PAUL: They're clean.

DOREEN: Go and wash them.

Exit PAUL.

EDDIE: I'll make some custard.

Exit EDDIE.

DOREEN: That shirt's not as nice. I like the other one better, it suits you better, the colour's better.

Scene 5

STUART, NICKY and GARY. STUART and NICKY are lying on their backs, NICKY is drinking a can of lager, GARY is sitting on a football.

GARY: I wanted him to marry her, I was only a kid. I didn't know she was alcoholic, she just smelt nice. She's alright, we have a laugh.

NICKY offers the can to STUART.

NICKY: Finish it if you like.

STUART: Oh right, ta.

NICKY drops back onto his back and looks up.

STUART drinks.

NICKY: It's all blue.

STUART: You finished the beer, that was my beer, I bought that beer.

NICKY: So get another one.

STUART: I haven't got any money.

NICKY: Gary's got money.

GARY: No I can't, it's me mam's.

STUART: You drank my beer.

NICKY: Stop going on, will you?

Silence.

STUART: Where were you last night?

NICKY: You're like an old woman.

STUART: No I'm not. Where were you?

NICKY: Out. Just enough for a can of lager.

GARY: It's her Giro, she'll kill me.

STUART crushes the can and throws it away.

STUART: You drank my beer.

Silence.

NICKY: Women float easier than men.

STUART: Bollocks.

NICKY clips STUART over the head.

NICKY: Go on, just a fiver.

STUART: How's your dad, Nicky?

NICKY: A fiver won't hurt.

STUART: Where were you last night?

NICKY: Watching the telly. Just a fiver.

STUART: No you weren't, I called round.

NICKY: I must have popped out to get a pint of milk.

STUART: I called round twice and you still weren't there.

NICKY: It was a big pint of milk. Who are you, my mum?

STUART: No.

NICKY: I was out.

STUART: Your dad didn't look very happy.

NICKY: (*To GARY.*) Come on, a fiver, she won't miss a fiver, that's all.

GARY: Oh, alright. (*He gives NICKY a fiver.*)

NICKY: Thanks, pal.

STUART: He doesn't get on with his dad.

NICKY: At least I know who my dad is. So, how's your sister?

GARY: Yeah, alright.

NICKY: When am I going to meet her?

Enter EDDIE. NICKY blocks his way.

Hello Eddie. Don't mind if we call you Eddie, do you? Where have you been to, Eddie?

EDDIE: Work.

NICKY: Where are you going?

EDDIE: Home.

NICKY: He's going home.

STUART: To his wife.

NICKY: What are you having for tea?

EDDIE tries to pass them but they block him.

EDDIE: Come on, boys.

NICKY: Please.

EDDIE: Please.

NICKY and STUART don't move.

NICKY: Me and Stuart have been playing football with Gary.

GARY: Hello, Mister Jackson.

EDDIE: Gary.

NICKY: What are you having for tea?

EDDIE: I don't know – chops.

NICKY: Chops.

STUART: I love chops.

NICKY: He eats anything, you're a pig, aren't you?

STUART: Yeah, I'm a pig.

EDDIE tries to pass. NICKY puts his arm round EDDIE.

NICKY: We're going for a drink, come for a drink with us.

EDDIE: No thanks.

NICKY takes his arm away from EDDIE.

NICKY: Oh I see, like that is it.

STUART: She won't let him.

NICKY: How is your wife?

EDDIE: Yeah, alright, she's alright.

NICKY: Just the one, you and us, come on.

EDDIE: No, honest lads – I have to get home.

NICKY: She can't be trusted.

STUART: She'll shag anyone.

NICKY: Don't be disgusting.

NICKY slaps STUART over the head.

Go on, Eddie, give him a slap.

STUART: Yeah, slap me.

EDDIE: No.

NICKY: It's true then.

EDDIE: I have to go home.

NICKY: She'll shag anything in trousers that looks like a man.

STUART: Yeah.

EDDIE: You've been drinking.

NICKY: Are you saying I can't have a drink?

EDDIE: No.

STUART: His family don't drink.

NICKY: They don't like people enjoying themselves.

STUART: They like the police.

NICKY: They drink tea.

STUART: Do you drink tea, Eddie?

EDDIE: I have to go home.

STUART: Do you like tea, well do you like it.

NICKY: So now we can't have a drink, you're telling me
I can't have a drink. You and your bloody family. I hate
your fucking guts Jackson, what are you going to do
about it?

EDDIE: I have to go home.

NICKY and STUART block his way.

Silence.

NICKY steps to one side.

Exit EDDIE.

NICKY: (*Shouting after EDDIE.*) I'm going to smash all
your windows Eddie and burn your house down, burn
your house while you're sleeping in it.

STUART: He's going to burn you, man.

NICKY: You deserve burning, man.

STUART: Burn grandad, burn.

NICKY: Burn in your sleep. Enjoy your chops, Eddie.

Silence.

What's the matter with you?

GARY: I cut my lip shaving.

NICKY: And another thing I don't fancy about being a
grandad, you go all saggy.

Enter JOHN.

JOHN: You leave my dad alone right, you hear, you
hear me, you hear – what's he done, he's done nothing

so leave him alone, leave him alone – you hear, you hear – he's got a bad heart he can't be doing with it, none of it, any of it – you leave him, just leave us alone.

NICKY: We never touched him.

JOHN: You leave my dad alone I'm telling you, you hear – leave him alone. Right?

NICKY: Right.

STUART: Right.

JOHN: Just leave us alone – he hasn't done anything, we haven't done anything.

STUART: Come on, let's get a bag of chips.

NICKY: He's hungry.

STUART: I want a kebab and chips.

NICKY: He likes burgers best. Do you like burgers, Johnny? I like burgers.

STUART: I love the smell of hot dogs.

NICKY: He had two Whoppas in Burger King last night, one after the other, and then he came out walked over the road straight into Macdonalds and has a Big Mac with fries. What are you looking at Johnny, what the bloody hell are you looking at? Don't look at me like that. What are you looking at? What are you bloody looking at, don't look at me like that, what gives you the right to bloody look at me like that, stop looking at me – what are you on – what you looking at, stop looking at me man, stop fucking looking at me?

JOHN: Don't talk to me like that.

NICKY: No, alright I won't.

NICKY throws a dummy head butt at JOHN.

NICKY and STUART laugh.

No hard feelings like, mate.

NICKY offers his hand for JOHN to shake.

It's only a bit of fun.

STUART: Yeah, no hard feelings.

STUART offers his hand for JOHN to shake.

JOHN shakes NICKY's hand.

JOHN shakes STUART's hand.

NICKY: Come on, let's get a bag of chips.

NICKY turns to go.

STUART head butts JOHN and kicks him to the ground. JOHN curls up into a ball and STUART continues kicking him. NICKY joins in.

GARY watches.

Enter EDDIE.

NICKY and STUART continue to kick JOHN.

EDDIE does nothing, he looks on. NICKY stops kicking and pulls STUART off.

STUART: Are you looking for help? Forget it, Dad, nobody helps any more.

STUART lands one final blow to JOHN's head and stamps on JOHN's outstretched wrist.

Exit NICKY and STUART.

End of Act One.

ACT TWO

Scene 6

NICKY and STUART.

STUART: It's cold. I'm cold We can't stop here.

NICKY: It's not safe on the road.

STUART: I hate trees. I hate the countryside.

NICKY: They were your mates, you said they would help.

STUART: How was I to know? It's not my fault, you can't blame me, I wasn't to know – it's not my fault.

Silence.

At least they gave us a bottle of whiskey.

STUART drinks from the bottle of whiskey.

We can go to my gran's.

NICKY: Oh yeah.

STUART: Yeah.

NICKY: It's miles away, we're miles away from anywhere.

STUART: We should catch a bus.

NICKY: I haven't got any money, have you got money? I spent all my money on getting to your mates.

STUART: My gran'll put us up, she likes me.

He gives the bottle to NICKY.

Finish it.

NICKY drinks.

I'm hungry.

NICKY: You're always hungry.

STUART: No, no, really hungry, I could eat an ox.

NICKY throws the bottle away.

Can you feel it?

NICKY: What?

STUART: Shut your eyes.

NICKY: Feel what?

STUART: Just shut your eyes and don't think anything.

NICKY shuts his eyes.

Don't think anything. Clear your head of all thoughts. So you're thinking nothing.

Silence.

Can you feel it?

NICKY begins to grin.

Can you feel it?

NICKY: Yeah.

STUART: Yeah.

NICKY: Yeah.

They both laugh.

STUART: I'm up man, really really up, I'm buzzing. I'm not drunk.

NICKY: It's the cold.

STUART: Too much air.

NICKY: I can smell your feet.

STUART: No that's the country.

STUART farts. They both laugh. NICKY is unable to stop laughing.

What, what you laughing at?

NICKY holds his sides and rolls over.

Stop laughing will you.

NICKY: It hurts, oh it hurts.

NICKY gains control of himself.

STUART: My head feels like a helicopter.

NICKY: I have to sign on tomorrow.

STUART: Yeah?

NICKY: Yeah.

They both laugh.

STUART: It's spinning. I'm never going to sleep again.

NICKY: I'm never going to sign on again.

STUART: He'll never walk again.

They laugh.

I'd be good in a war.

NICKY: Oh yeah.

STUART: Yeah.

NICKY: Is that why you ran out of the Kentucky Fried Chicken the other week, when those Asian lads started throwing chairs about?

STUART: That was different, I'm talking about a real life war zone situation.

NICKY: He shouldn't have come at us like that – first his dad and then him, he provoked it, it was provocation.

STUART: Yeah. He's scum. The whole family are scum. We did everyone a favour, you'll see.

NICKY: It was self-defence.

STUART: No.

NICKY: No. We kicked the shit out of him.

STUART: Yeah.

NICKY: Yeah.

They laugh.

STUART: This is just like being in the Scouts.

NICKY: I didn't know you were a Scout.

STUART: No, I wasn't. I keep seeing the way he fell. In slow motion.

STUART reacts in slow motion to punches being thrown at him, falling to the ground, being kicked and curling up into a ball. All done in slow motion and enjoyed very much.

NICKY: Give us a fag.

STUART: I'm all out.

Silence.

I feel like a shag.

NICKY: You don't look like a shag.

STUART: He deserved to die.

NICKY: If it hadn't been us it would have been somebody else – you only have to touch him and he starts crying.

STUART: Yeah.

NICKY: Bawling his eyes out.

STUART: Cry baby.

NICKY: I'm not sorry.

STUART: No me neither. I do, I feel like a shag.

NICKY: Too much sex shrinks the brain.

STUART: You haven't got anything to worry about then.

NICKY: No, it's true – scientists in China have done this experiment – they measured the size of a male rat's brain before sex and after and found that it had shrunk.

STUART: How did they measure its brain?

NICKY: I don't know, measuring equipment. It's true, honest.

STUART: What about the female rat?

NICKY: What about it?

STUART: What about its brain?

NICKY: They weren't measuring that.

STUART: Why not?

NICKY: Because they weren't.

STUART: Alright.

Silence.

NICKY: We'll go to your gran's.

STUART: Yeah. I'm her favourite.

NICKY: Give us a fag.

STUART: I haven't got any.

Silence.

My trainers have split.

NICKY: It'll be manslaughter.

STUART: Nobody likes him, nobody likes any of them.

NICKY: What else can they do us for?

STUART: Murder.

NICKY: That girl in America killed a baby and got off with manslaughter, she got off with nothing. If you can drop a baby on its head and get away with it, what are they going to do to us?

STUART: Yeah, but it was a baby.

NICKY: He was old enough to look after himself.

STUART: Nobody gives a toss about babies.

NICKY: They can't do us for murder.

STUART: I don't care. I can handle whatever they throw at me. I don't want to go to prison but I will if I have to. You'll be alright, you've been before.

NICKY: Yeah.

STUART: (*Looking at his shoes.*) They have, they've split.

NICKY: We could go to London.

STUART: I'm not going to London.

NICKY: They'd never find us in London.

STUART: I don't like London.

NICKY: You've never been.

STUART: Neither have you. You want to go to London.

NICKY: Yeah.

STUART: Go to London.

NICKY: Right, I will.

STUART: Go to bloody London, see if I care. You don't even know where we are, we're lost.

NICKY: I'm not lost.

STUART: So where are we then?

NICKY: In a field.

STUART: Which way's north?

NICKY: What for?

STUART: You don't know.

NICKY: I know which way's north, I don't have to tell you which way's north to prove I know which way's north.

STUART: Oh yeah.

NICKY: Yeah.

STUART: Yeah.

STUART sits.

I thought you were going to London.

NICKY: We'll go to your gran's.

STUART: She's got a loft.

Exit STUART and NICKY.

Scene 7

DOREEN centre stage sitting on a chair two tablets in her hand.

STUART downstage right sitting on a chair. To one side of his chair a pair of trainers, shoelaces and a belt. He is smoking

DOREEN: The police had just left. I was standing at the gate. A young boy in the road shouted, 'We've killed your son, now we'll kill you.'

She looks at the tablets.

He said they would help – so I can sleep. I can't sleep. I don't want to sleep. He said they would help.

Enter HORSLEY downstage right.

HORSLEY: Are you alright? Do you want anything to read?

STUART: No, thanks.

HORSLEY: We've got comics.

STUART: No.

HORSLEY goes to exit.

I need the toilet.

HORSLEY: Come on then.

Exit STUART followed by HORSLEY.

Enter EDDIE with a glass of water.

EDDIE: I got you some water. Come on. You've got to, he said, the doctor said. He said it would help.

DOREEN: Everywhere I look it's John. It's not empty. The house is full of John.

EDDIE offers her the glass of water.

EDDIE: You have to.

DOREEN: I should be dead.

EDDIE: The doctor said.

DOREEN: It's all my fault, it's all my fault, everything – it's all my fault – I should have done nothing, I should have kept quiet, I shouldn't have interfered, I should have ignored it – the shouting the fighting the stealing the burning the fear the misery the bullying the hate – I should have kept my mouth shut, I should have done nothing, I shouldn't have interfered. If I'd done nothing. I remember saying to a policeman, 'What will it take, does one of my children have to die to put a stop to all this.' It would have been better not to have had children.

EDDIE touches her shoulder.

Don't – don't.

EDDIE offers her the glass.

EDDIE: For me, do it for me.

DOREEN: I don't want a tablet.

EDDIE: It'll help.

DOREEN: I don't want a tablet. I want to die, I wish I was dead.

EDDIE: It's alright, you'll be alright.

DOREEN: I wish I was dead.

EDDIE: For me.

DOREEN: I've got nothing.

Silence.

Where's Paul, I don't know where Paul is, where's Paul?

EDDIE: Up in his room.

DOREEN: Don't let him go out, you won't let him out, I can't let him out.

EDDIE: He's not going out.

DOREEN: You'll tell me if he does?

EDDIE: Take your tablet.

DOREEN: You won't let him out without telling me, you'll tell me?

EDDIE offers the glass of water and she takes it.

Oh God – I shouldn't be like this, I know I shouldn't but I can't help it. I'll push him away, he'll go away he'll leave me and then I'll have no one I'll have nothing. I'll crush him, I'm falling apart – he'll leave me, I'm driving him away – it's my nerves – I couldn't stand it I couldn't bear the pain – I'm driving him away, I shouldn't be like this I know I shouldn't. but I can't help it – I couldn't stand to lose him as well.

EDDIE: It's alright, we're alright, he's alright he's up in his room. Now take your tablet like the doctor said, he was a nice lad.

DOREEN: Yes he was a nice boy.

EDDIE: The doctor was a nice boy.

DOREEN takes the tablets and drinks the water.

EDDIE takes the glass off her

DOREEN: Thank you.

Enter PAUL with his jacket on.

PAUL: I'm going out.

DOREEN: Where are you going?

PAUL: I won't be long.

DOREEN: Where are you going?

PAUL: Just out.

DOREEN: When are you coming back?

PAUL: I don't know. I'm not sure. I'll be back.

DOREEN: You'll be back?

PAUL: Yeah, I'll be back.

DOREEN: For your tea?

PAUL: I don't know.

DOREEN: But you'll be back?

PAUL: Mam. Look, I've said, haven't I?

DOREEN: You go out, go out and enjoy yourself.

PAUL: I don't enjoy myself.

DOREEN: I want you to enjoy yourself.

PAUL: How can I enjoy myself?

DOREEN: You go out and enjoy yourself, you leave us here, we're alright, we can manage – you go out... you go out – it's my nerves, I'm falling apart – I wish they were dead – I do, I wish God would strike both those boys dead – It's the only thing I've got to hang onto that keeps me alive – I know it's wicked, I know it's evil, I should forgive, I can't forgive – I wish those two boys were dead and you'll go out and you'll leave me and you'll never come back and I won't know how to go on living and you'll be dead –

PAUL: Stop it, Mam, stop it.

DOREEN: You'll be dead and I'll wish it was me.

PAUL: I'm coming back, I'll be back I always come back – I can't stay here, I have to go out I have to get out, I can't stop in.

EDDIE: I'll put the kettle on.

Exit EDDIE.

DOREEN: You go out and enjoy yourself.

PAUL: I'm not going out to enjoy myself. I'm going out for a walk. How can I enjoy myself, I can't enjoy myself they hate our bloody guts.

59

DOREEN: You never used to swear.

PAUL: What does it matter, nothing matters, it doesn't matter, nothing matters any more nothing, nothing, nothing.

DOREEN: You shouldn't ought to have sworn. I'm your mother.

Enter EDDIE.

EDDIE: You want a cup of tea, son?

PAUL: No, no thanks, Dad.

Silence.

I'm going out.

DOREEN: You'll be back for your tea.

EDDIE: Leave the boy alone.

PAUL: I'll be alright.

EDDIE: He'll be alright.

DOREEN: What do you know.

PAUL: Please Mam, don't, don't – I'm just going for a walk, I'll be ten minutes, I'm just going down to the shops for a packet of fags and then I'll be back.

DOREEN: You're coming back?

PAUL: I'm coming back.

DOREEN: You'll be back for your tea?

PAUL: Yes.

He kisses her.

I'll be back. Do you want anything, Dad?

EDDIE: No, no thanks son.

Exit PAUL.

Silence.

You want tea? I want tea. What do you want?

DOREEN: I couldn't bear it, I couldn't bear the pain I know I shouldn't be like this but I can't help it and I'm driving him away – I'm falling apart inside, I'm disintegrating.

EDDIE: I'll make some tea. You want tea? I want tea.

Enter STUART downstage right and sits on a chair.

DOREEN: I can't help it, I can't help myself.

EDDIE: It's alright, it's alright.

DOREEN: I'm sorry.

EDDIE. It's alright.

DOREEN: I should forgive but I can't. I want to see them in hell.

EDDIE: I'll make the tea.

Exit EDDIE.

Enter HORSLEY, a newspaper in his jacket pocket.

HORSLEY: Do you like football?

STUART: Yeah.

HORSLEY: I like rugby. The beautiful thing about football is that any fool can become an expert after watching only half a minute

Silence.

Your mate.

Silence.

He'll be alright.

HORSLEY lights a cigarette,

Exit DOREEN.

Put your shoes on, Stuart. Your feet smell.

STUART: I can't smell anything.

HORSLEY: That's because they're your feet.

STUART: I've always had bad feet.

HORSLEY: Put your shoes on, Stuart.

STUART puts on his trainers.

STUART: I can't breath down there. It does my head in. I didn't do anything, it wasn't me, honest, it wasn't my fault I haven't done anything.

HORSLEY: And the belt.

HORSLEY sits. He takes the rolled-up newspaper out of his jacket pocket and watches STUART.

STUART puts on his belt.

STUART: What about the laces?

HORSLEY: In the bin.

STUART puts the laces in the bin. He sits.

Silence.

HORSLEY reads his paper.

STUART: I haven't done anything.

HORSLEY: You haven't got anything to worry about then.

STUART: I didn't do anything.

STUART cries.

HORSLEY: What? What is it, what are you crying for? What is it, Stuart? Is it John? Is it John you're crying for? Here. (*He gives STUART a hanky.*)

STUART takes the hanky and wipes his eyes and blows his nose.

Have you got any kids? I've got kids. I'm a dad. This sort of thing makes you think. Some people aren't fit to have kids – but how do you know, how do you know who's fit and who isn't?

STUART doesn't know what to do with the hanky.

Keep it.

STUART: Thanks. You won't lock me up again, not yet you said.

HORSLEY: I said nothing.

STUART: You told me to put my shoes on.

HORSLEY: Your feet smell. What is it, Stuart, what is it you're scared of? D'you think I'm going to hit you?

STUART: Yes – no, Mister Horsley, sir.

HORSLEY: Stop taking the piss.

STUART: I'm not.

HORSLEY: You are. Do you like taking the piss?

STUART: No.

HORSLEY: That's not what I heard. That's not what your mate said. What then, what is it, what are you scared of?

STUART: Nothing, mister Horsley, sir.

HORSLEY: Stop taking the piss.

STUART: I'm not.

HORSLEY: You are.

Silence.

I like you, Stuart – that's why you're up here, why you're not locked up downstairs. I like you.

STUART: I didn't do anything, I haven't done anything.

HORSLEY: Your mate.

STUART: I feel sick.

HORSLEY: He just opens his mouth and it doesn't stop.

STUART: I feel sick.

HORSLEY: He'll be alright, he can look after himself.

STUART: He said he wasn't feeling well, he had a bad stomach, I was looking after him, I couldn't leave him, I was just looking after him.

HORSLEY: In your gran's loft.

STUART: All day.

HORSLEY: So why didn't you try telling him a joke?

STUART: I didn't do anything, I haven't done anything.

HORSLEY: It's alright, Stuart, I'm sorry – I'm sorry it's just I get very emotional when it comes to children, young people – you know.

STUART: It's not my fault, it wasn't my fault, I haven't done anything.

Silence.

HORSLEY goes to exit.

You'll be back, you're coming back.

HORSLEY: I'm going to get a doughnut. And then I'll be back. And then I'm going home, I'm going home to bed. Do you like doughnuts? Do you want a doughnut?

Enter DOREEN. She sits on a chair centre stage.

I'll tell you what, if they've got two I'll bring you one back, I can't say fairer than that, can I?

STUART: No. Don't shut the door – leave it open, just a bit, leave the door open.

HORSLEY: I'm sorry Stuart, I can't do that.

HORSLEY goes to exit.

Oh, by the way – your mam and dad rang, just to say they moved but they forgot to leave an address.

Exit HORSLEY.

DOREEN: I don't feel so bad today. I feel good enough to clean a window. Last week I felt like dying but today I feel well enough to clean a window.

Scene 8

DOREEN and PAUL.

PAUL: I'm not going back to college. I've got a job. I got a job. In a cafe. In town.

DOREEN: How much will that pay?

PAUL: Enough.

DOREEN: That won't pay much.

PAUL: It's enough. I don't need much.

DOREEN: That's right, throw your life away.

PAUL: No, I'm not.

DOREEN: Ruin your life.

PAUL: I can't go back.

DOREEN: Why not?

PAUL: Because I can't.

DOREEN: You're going back.

PAUL: It's never right is it, whatever I want is never right, whatever I do or say it's never right – what do you want, I can't do anything – I go out the door and you're on at me, where am I going, who am I seeing, when am I coming back – and now, when I say I don't want to go, that I'm stopping, that I'm not going, you want me to go – What do you want?

DOREEN: You'll go back to university and you'll thank me for it.

PAUL: I've rented a room.

DOREEN: Well you can unrent it.

PAUL: In town.

DOREEN: You live here.

PAUL: It'll save on bus fares.

DOREEN: You won't be able to afford it.

PAUL: I'll save on bus fares.

DOREEN: You live here.

PAUL: It's near work.

DOREEN: You won't manage.

PAUL: I'll manage.

DOREEN: You're going back to university.

PAUL: No Mam, no – I need time, I have to sort myself out.

DOREEN: You're not leaving home.

PAUL: I have to.

DOREEN: Over my dead body.

PAUL: I'm going, I'm leaving and that's all there is to it.

DOREEN: I'll stab you with a knife first.

PAUL: It's always the same – whatever I do I can't win, whatever I do it's not right unless it's what you want me to do and I go round and round in my head trying to please you and it's never enough, I'm never enough – Alright, alright, I'm not going I won't go. Is that what you want me to say?

DOREEN: Yes.

PAUL: I've said it. I'll get up one morning and I'll walk out that door without telling you and I won't come back.

DOREEN: You're leaving because of me.

PAUL: No, I'm leaving because I can't stop, because of me.

Enter EDDIE.

DOREEN: I'm driving you away.

PAUL: No Mam, no.

DOREEN: It's all my fault.

PAUL: I can't stay. You don't need me, she doesn't need me. She's got you, you've got dad, you've got each other, you don't need me.

DOREEN: You don't know what I need.

PAUL: I'm going and you can't stop me.

DOREEN: Oh yes I can.

PAUL: How, how can you stop me?

EDDIE: Just pack it in, the pair of you.

PAUL: You can't stop me.

DOREEN: Over my dead body.

Exit DOREEN.

EDDIE: What's going on, what have you done to your mother?

PAUL: Nothing. I can't stop, I have to go – she won't let me go.

EDDIE: You want to go, Paul, you want to leave, Paul?

PAUL: Yes I do.

EDDIE: Then bloody do it and stop making such a song and dance.

Enter DOREEN with a bread knife.

DOREEN: I'll stab you, I'll maim you.

PAUL: Go on then.

EDDIE: I said pack it in.

PAUL: You wouldn't.

DOREEN: Oh yes I would.

EDDIE: That's enough, I've had enough.

PAUL: It's all so, you're so… I walk in this house and – you won't let go, she won't let go – not me, not John, not anything – the suffering, suffering in silence, all dying in silence.

PAUL makes to go.

DOREEN: You're not going.

PAUL: I'm going.

EDDIE: Put the knife down, Doreen.

PAUL: Go on then, I dare you.

DOREEN: I'll stab you.

EDDIE: Put the knife down.

PAUL: I'm going.

DOREEN: I'll kill you!

> *DOREEN lowers his knife and cries.*

> *EDDIE takes the knife and helps her to sit.*

There's nothing we can do. All we can do is pray.

PAUL: For what? What for? There is no God.

DOREEN: He's trying to kill me.

PAUL: What, God?

DOREEN: You want to kill me.

PAUL: After this there's nothing.

DOREEN: You're killing me.

PAUL: And what about John? What kind of a God did that? What God? There is no God.

DOREEN: I'm being punished.

EDDIE: Just leave your mother alone.

PAUL: God did nothing, you did nothing. (*He exits.*)

> *Enter NICKY downstage right and sits. He neatly places a pair of trainers to one side of his chair.*

EDDIE: He's old enough to do what he wants, Doreen. We have to let him go.

DOREEN: I'll go and see that he's alright.

EDDIE: No. Leave him.

> *EDDIE sits.*

I keep having these dreams.

DOREEN: You look tired.

EDDIE: I am tired.

DOREEN: You go to bed.

EDDIE: I can't sleep.

DOREEN: You sleep.

EDDIE: I can't. I keep having these dreams.

DOREEN: I'll go and see that he's alright.

Exit DOREEN. EDDIE remains sitting.

Enter HORSLEY downstage right.

NICKY: I drink too much right and I get mellow, he drinks too much and all he wants to do is fight.

HORSLEY: He's a fighter alright.

NICKY: I'm not saying that I've never had a fight or that I don't fight –

HORSLEY: You're always fighting.

NICKY: Not always, mainly with my brothers.

HORSLEY: How's your cell?

NICKY shrugs.

Exit EDDIE.

NICKY: Can I put my shoes on?

HORSLEY: No.

NICKY: The floor's cold.

HORSLEY: You've got a reputation for it.

NICKY: What.

HORSLEY: Fighting.

NICKY: Can I smoke?

HORSLEY: No.

NICKY: Yeah well, that was in my younger years – since then I've gained some control. I've learned to curb the anger, I've just learned to beat the shit out of other things and not people.

HORSLEY: What about John?

NICKY: Look, I'm not pretending I liked him, nor his family, I'm not even sorry he's dead – a bunch of arseholes – but I never touched him, why would I bother?

HORSLEY: For fun.

NICKY: Oh yeah, he was a right laugh.

HORSLEY: So, Stuart's mates wouldn't have you and you had to walk back? Twelve miles.

NICKY: Can I smoke?

HORSLEY: Long walk.

NICKY: Can I smoke?

HORSLEY: No. So, you get a bit mad when you drink.

NICKY: No.

HORSLEY: Angry then?

NICKY: No. Yeah, I've had fights. I've had fights with some of my best mates.

HORSLEY: We've got witnesses.

Silence.

NICKY: His dad. Yeah well, he would say that, wouldn't he?

HORSLEY: What, say what?

Silence.

NICKY: It was one of my mates birthday right, so we shaved his eyebrows off – well we did one as a laugh and it looked so stupid we had to do the other one.

HORSLEY: You think this is funny?

NICKY: No. Are you going to charge me then? What are you charging me for? You touch me and I'll have you for assault.

HORSLEY: Don't come any of that barrack room lawyer stuff with me, son.

NICKY: You can't do this.

HORSLEY: I can do what I want.

Silence.

NICKY runs his hand through his hair.

NICKY: I hate my hair. I'd have it all shaved off but for the scars on my head.

HORSLEY: Have you got any sisters?

NICKY: No.

HORSLEY: It must have something to do with your mother then.

NICKY: What?

HORSLEY: You, wearing your hair like that.

NICKY: I want it shaved, but I'm talking about serious scars, man. Dirty great scars all over my head from when I came off a motorbike and ripped open my head.

HORSLEY: Stuart's a bit of a talker isn't he, once he get's going.

NICKY: I don't know.

HORSLEY: Don't know much, do you?

NICKY: No.

Silence.

HORSLEY: Yeah.

HORSLEY makes a note in his notebook.

NICKY: What's that you're writing?

HORSLEY: Nothing.

NICKY: Is it about me?

HORSLEY: It's private. I'm thirsty. I'd like to be sat down in a pub now, with a pint of beer. I like beer. Do you like beer?

NICKY: Special Brew.

HORSLEY: There's blood on your trainers.

NICKY looks at the shoes next to his chair.

NICKY: I can't see any blood.

HORSLEY: The ones you threw away.

NICKY: I cut myself shaving.

HORSLEY: John's blood. How did it get there?

NICKY: I don't know. Look, I wouldn't have left his blood on my shoe if I'd have thought it was his blood, would I?

HORSLEY: Wouldn't you?

NICKY: No, I'm not stupid, you know.

HORSLEY: The blood is in the stitches, you can't see it.

Silence.

NICKY: Just charge me. Charge me and get on with it. I'm not saying anything, I've got nothing to say.

Silence.

What, what do you want me to say?

Silence.

You want to see if we're mad don't you, to see if there was anything playing in our heads when it happened. He just fell, he fell and hit his head on the ground.

Scene 9

EDDIE and HORSLEY. EDDIE is sitting on a chair centre stage.

EDDIE: I went outside to stop it and when I got there John was on the ground and they were kicking him and I couldn't move. I didn't believe it was happening, I couldn't move, I was frozen to the spot, I couldn't do anything. And they stopped and he said, 'Are you looking for help?', and he was calm, for the first time calm, like he was really asking – and he said 'Forget it dad, nobody helps any more.' And then the small one –

HORSLEY: Stuart.

EDDIE nods.

EDDIE: Stuart. He kicked John in the head again and stamped down hard, a hard crack on his wrist – like it was an extra little something, a present – a going away present – and I heard his bone snap. And I couldn't move.

Exit HORSLEY.

Enter DOREEN with a sandwich on a small plate. She gives the plate to EDDIE.

DOREEN: There was a bit of cheese.

She sits.

Did you want pickle? There isn't any pickle. Eat your sandwich.

EDDIE: You should see the doctor.

DOREEN: I'm not well enough.

EDDIE: He'll give you something.

DOREEN: I don't want to be a burden. The woman up the road's written it down, it's on a piece of paper, that if anything happens to her, that she can't manage – she doesn't want her son to come back and look after her, she wants to be put in an old peoples home, she doesn't want to be a burden – I don't want to be a burden.

Silence.

EDDIE: They won't let you in an old people's home.

DOREEN: Why not?

EDDIE: You're not old enough.

Silence.

DOREEN: Eat your sandwich.

Silence.

Enter JOHN.

JOHN: A local man and youth who kicked and punched to death a teenager in his front garden on the Gladstone Estate were yesterday jailed for his murder. Nicholas Tanner, aged twenty two, was jailed for life and Stuart Earnshaw, seventeen, was sentenced to be detained at Her Majesty's pleasure. John Jackson aged seventeen, had been trying to persuade them to stop abusing his father. He was attacked with a volley of punches and kicks by Tanner and Earnshaw. The attack, which continued as the teenager lay unconscious on the ground, left him unable to defend himself. He eventually choked to death on his own blood.

DOREEN: Eat your sandwich.

EDDIE: I'm not hungry.

JOHN: His father who was standing just feet away, said the two treated his son's head like a football. Within two minutes they had fled leaving John dead. Tanner and Earnshaw admitted that they had carried out the attack, both denied they had intended to kill John. Nicky Tanner held his head in his hands and fought back the tears as the murder verdicts were delivered. Stuart Earnshaw mouthed 'No way' and shouted to his family 'Don't worry' before being led away. At a press conference after the case, Doreen Jackson, forty nine, said: 'Eight years ago I started a petition to deal with local hooligans on the Estate, which made my family victims of a hate campaign. Sometimes I wonder if I had kept my mouth shut would my son still be alive. There have been threats ever since my son died. The harassment hasn't stopped. We have no protection'.

EDDIE: Later, I'll have it later.

Exit EDDIE.

The loud crash of a window smashing.

MAN's VOICE: (*Offstage.*) You're dead Jackson, you're all dead.

Exit JOHN.

Scene 10

DOREEN.

Music offstage.

She is sorting a laundry basket of mixed washing, folding towels tea towels and shirts and placing them in a neat pile on the seat of a chair next to her: leaving an assortment of socks and underwear in the basket.

The music stops. Enter EDDIE in overcoat.

EDDIE: You left the radio on.

DOREEN: I was listening to that.

EDDIE unbuttons his coat.

EDDIE: Paul not here yet?

DOREEN: No, he's late. I had your Auntie June on the phone today.

EDDIE: Oh aye, what did she have to say?

EDDIE takes off his coat.

DOREEN: She says, she didn't expect to make it as far as mid November, but now that she has she doesn't hold out much hope for December.

Exit EDDIE.

DOREEN puts the pile of folded laundry into the basket.

She was ringing to wish us a Merry Christmas, just in case she didn't make it that far.

Enter EDDIE.

EDDIE: What did you say?

DOREEN: I said, if she could last out to the New Year we might get across to sea her.

EDDIE: Aye.

DOREEN: What time is it?

EDDIE: Twelve thirty.

DOREEN: He's late.

EDDIE: It'll be traffic.

DOREEN: I used to love the winter when I was a child, sliding to school.

EDDIE: How's your limp?

DOREEN: I don't limp.

EDDIE: You limp.

DOREEN: It's my bones, they're crumbling.

EDDIE: Your bones aren't crumbling.

PAUL: (*Offstage.*) Mam, Dad.

DOREEN: He's late.

Enter PAUL With a bunch of flowers and a bag.

Oh, he's got flowers.

PAUL: They're for John.

EDDIE: How was the traffic son?

PAUL: Yeah, alright – the bus got stuck in a traffic jam, just up past the by-pass.

DOREEN: They're lovely.

PAUL: I thought I might go up after dinner. I got you a box of chocolates.

DOREEN: You spoil me.

PAUL: I like spoiling you.

He gives her a box of chocolates.

EDDIE: The traffic's got worse since they built that by-pass.

PAUL: They're Belgian.

DOREEN: You let yourself in, you've still got your key.

EDDIE: I won't deny that it eased the congestion at first – there's too many cars on the road, that's the problem.

DOREEN: You've had your haircut.

PAUL: Don't start.

DOREEN: It's too short.

PAUL: You start and I'm going.

DOREEN: No, don't go.

PAUL: Of course I'm not going.

He kisses her on the cheek.

I haven't had my dinner yet.

DOREEN: It's good of you to come.

PAUL: No it's not, I like coming, I like seeing that you're alright.

DOREEN: You should put those in water, I'll put them in some water for you.

PAUL: No it's alright.

DOREEN: They'll curl up and die.

PAUL: I'll do it.

EDDIE: They reckon it might snow, it's warm enough to. I was out walking by the canal. Beautiful blue sky. And the sun on the water.

PAUL: I'll go and put these in water.

DOREEN: Where did you get your haircut?

PAUL: A barber's.

DOREEN: It's too short.

PAUL: I don't care, I just had whatever she said.

EDDIE: She?

PAUL: Yeah 'she', she was a woman, Dad.

DOREEN: Leave him alone.

EDDIE: You went to a barber's?

PAUL: I got my haircut.

DOREEN: It's good of you to come.

PAUL: No it's not, I like coming.

EDDIE: I don't know of any barbers where a woman works. You didn't go to a barbers, he didn't go to a barbers, he went to a woman's hairdressing salon.

PAUL: It was a shop where they cut hair.

DOREEN: It's too short, Paul.

EDDIE: Never let a woman cut your hair son.

PAUL: I was thinking of having it shaved.

DOREEN: You do and you'll be wearing a woolly hat when you come to visit us.

PAUL: I'll put these in water

Exit PAUL.

EDDIE: He went to a hairdresser's.

DOREEN: He's not eating.

EDDIE: Let's have one of your chocolates then.

DOREEN: He's not looking after himself.

EDDIE: Have a chocolate.

DOREEN: He's lost weight.

EDDIE: They're Belgian.

DOREEN: He's not eating.

EDDIE: Have a chocolate.

DOREEN: I don't want a chocolate, you have a chocolate.

EDDIE: They're your chocolates.

DOREEN: He's got rings under his eyes.

EDDIE: He bought them for you.

DOREEN: He brought them for all of us.

EDDIE: He bought them for you!

Enter PAUL.

PAUL: I've put them in water.

DOREEN: You said you'd ring.

PAUL: The bus got stuck.

DOREEN: You said you'd ring.

PAUL: There wasn't a phone.

DOREEN: You said you'd ring if you were going to be late.

PAUL: I was on the bus.

DOREEN: There's no need to shout.

PAUL: I'm not. Have a chocolate.

DOREEN: I'll have a biscuit.

She looks at EDDIE.

EDDIE: You want me to get you a biscuit. I'll get you a biscuit.

Exit EDDIE.

DOREEN: You're not looking after yourself.

PAUL: I'm alright. Don't Mam, don't.

Silence.

DOREEN: What do you want for your birthday?

PAUL: I don't.

DOREEN: Well you can't have nothing.

PAUL: I don't want anything. I'm never celebrating my birthday again. A mark of respect.

DOREEN: What do you want for Christmas?

PAUL: I don't know. I might go away.

DOREEN: Go away where.

PAUL: It's not decided.

DOREEN: You're not coming home for Christmas?

PAUL: Probably.

DOREEN: Probably will or probably won't?

PAUL: It's not decided.

DOREEN: Well let me know when you've decided.

PAUL: Yeah, I will.

DOREEN: My door is always open.

Enter EDDIE with a newspaper and a biscuit.

EDDIE: Here's your biscuit.

DOREEN: I'll have a chocolate.

EDDIE: You did that on purpose.

DOREEN: What?

EDDIE: I know you.

DOREEN: What, what have I done?

EDDIE: I'm not telling.

DOREEN offers EDDIE a chocolate.

Thank you.

He takes one.

PAUL and DOREEN take a chocolate.

They all put their chocolates in their mouth at the same time. They eat.

DOREEN: Mmmh.

EDDIE: Mmmh.

PAUL: Mmmh.

DOREEN: Delicious.

EDDIE: Very good.

DOREEN: He was sixteen stone and now look at him.

PAUL: You're not eating Dad.

EDDIE: I'm eating, what do you think this is, a mirage.

DOREEN: He's not eating.

EDDIE: She's stopped cooking.

DOREEN: No I haven't.

EDDIE: Spaghetti and rice, that's not cooking.

DOREEN: He wants meat all the time.

EDDIE: She's turned vegetarian.

DOREEN: I don't think it's right, killing all those animals
    – and he starts moaning.

EDDIE: I don't moan, I've never moaned.

DOREEN: You cook the dinner then.

EDDIE: I'm not cooking.

PAUL: I'll cook.

EDDIE: You can't cook, he can't cook.

PAUL: I'll cook. What are we having.

DOREEN: Ask your father, he did the shopping.

EDDIE: I couldn't think –

DOREEN: Tell him what you got.

EDDIE: I got what I always get when I can't think, I got chops – and a sausage roll for your mother.

PAUL: She's vegetarian.

EDDIE: I got her a sausage roll.

PAUL: Sausage, dad, sausage.

EDDIE: There's no meat in a sausage roll, they're all sawdust and bits.

DOREEN: I'll have it warmed up.

Exit PAUL.

Silence.

Life should mean life.

Music from offstage.

EDDIE: He's got the radio on.

DOREEN: I'll give him a hand with the veg.

EDDIE sits and opens his paper.

DOREEN goes to exit.

EDDIE: I'll do the gravy.

DOREEN: You can take that washing upstairs.

Exit DOREEN.

Exit EDDIE with the laundry basket.

Scene 11

PAUL and GARY, PAUL with a bunch of flowers.

GARY: Paul.

PAUL: Gary.

GARY: Where have you been?

PAUL: Home.

GARY: Where are you going?

PAUL: To see John.

GARY: Up the cemetery. I don't like cemeteries, full of dead people.

PAUL: They've broke his headstone.

GARY: Who've broke his headstone?

> *PAUL shrugs.*

> Vandals. No respect.

> *PAUL makes to go.*

> Got any fags?

PAUL: No.

GARY: Stop and have a fag with me, not in a hurry are you?

> *GARY blocks PAUL's exit.*

PAUL: No.

> *GARY offers PAUL a cigarette.*

GARY: Have a fag.

PAUL: No thanks.

GARY: Go on, enjoy yourself.

PAUL: I've given up.

GARY lights a cigarette

GARY: Nice flowers.

PAUL: Yeah.

GARY: You've been to see your mum?

PAUL: Yeah.

GARY: Nice, that's nice, I bet she likes that.

PAUL: Yeah she does.

Silence.

I have to go.

GARY: I haven't finished my fag yet.

Silence.

You live in town.

PAUL: Yeah.

GARY: Whereabouts in town?

PAUL: Over a launderette.

GARY: That's handy.

PAUL: Yeah, very.

GARY: What are you getting like that for?

PAUL: I have to go.

GARY: What about university?

PAUL: I didn't like it.

GARY: Yeah, full of students. I saw you on the telly. And your picture, in the papers. I might come into town and see you someday.

PAUL: I have to go, I have to get there before dark.

GARY: Why, what happens when it gets dark?

PAUL: They lock the gate.

GARY: Jump over the wall. Are you working?

PAUL: No.

GARY: Me neither.

PAUL: I was.

GARY: Oh yeah.

PAUL: Washing up.

GARY: I couldn't do it.

PAUL: Me neither.

They both laugh.

GARY: What are you laughing at?

PAUL: Nothing.

Silence.

GARY: Are you sure you won't have a fag?

PAUL: Yeah.

GARY: Not good enough for you.

PAUL: I've given up.

GARY: How do you pay your rent?

PAUL: Housing benefit.

GARY: That's lucky. I suppose you got it easy because of special circumstances.

PAUL: Yeah.

GARY: Special circumstances. I enjoyed reading about it in all the papers. The police wanted me to act as a witness but I had nothing to say, I didn't see anything. It wasn't a fair trial. They were just out to get them for whatever they could. I've seen Nicky. I go up and visit. It's every month, when I can. I like the bus ride – it's out in the country. I took him some fags. It'll go to appeal, what do you reckon?

Silence.

No. They've put Nicky's mum on drugs to calm her nerves. I suppose she'll want to visit when she gets better. I don't know how Stuart's doing. His gran's not well. Did you give your mum a bunch of flowers?

PAUL: No, box of chocolates.

GARY: Nice.

PAUL: Yeah.

GARY: You'd better be going then.

GARY makes way for PAUL.

It's getting dark.

PAUL: Yeah.

PAUL goes to exit.

GARY: You want to watch it mate, or your face is going to end up like your brother's.

The End.